BEHIND THE BRAND

MINECRAFT

BY SARA GREEN

BLASTOFF!
DISCOVERY

BELLWETHER MEDIA • MINNEAPOLIS, MN

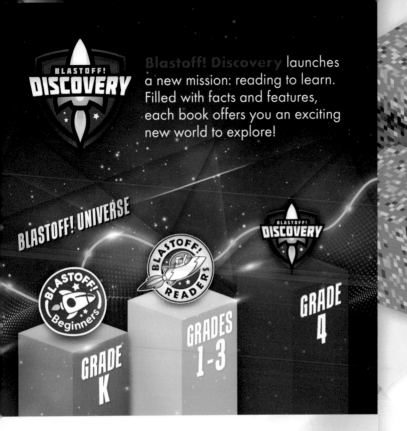

Blastoff! Discovery launches a new mission: reading to learn. Filled with facts and features, each book offers you an exciting new world to explore!

BLASTOFF! UNIVERSE

BLASTOFF! Beginners — GRADE K

BLASTOFF! READERS — GRADES 1-3

BLASTOFF! DISCOVERY — GRADE 4

This edition first published in 2023 by Bellwether Media, Inc.

No part of this publication may be reproduced in whole or in part without written permission of the publisher.
For information regarding permission, write to Bellwether Media, Inc., Attention: Permissions Department,
6012 Blue Circle Drive, Minnetonka, MN 55343.

Library of Congress Cataloging-in-Publication Data

Names: Green, Sara, 1964- author.
Title: Minecraft / by Sara Green.
Description: Minneapolis, MN : Bellwether Media, 2023. | Series: Blastoff! discovery. Behind the brand | Includes bibliographical references and index. | Audience: Ages 7-13 | Audience: Grades 4-6 | Summary: "Engaging images accompany information about Minecraft. The combination of high-interest subject matter and narrative text is intended for students in grades 3 through 8"– Provided by publisher.
Identifiers: LCCN 2022049465 (print) | LCCN 2022049466 (ebook) | ISBN 9798886871425 (library binding) | ISBN 9798886872088 (paperback) | ISBN 9798886872682 (ebook)
Subjects: LCSH: Minecraft (Game)–Juvenile literature.
Classification: LCC GV1469.35.M535 G74 2023 (print) | LCC GV1469.35.M535 (ebook) | DDC 794.8092 [B]–dc23/eng/20221017
LC record available at https://lccn.loc.gov/2022049465
LC ebook record available at https://lccn.loc.gov/2022049466

Editor: Betsy Rathburn   Designer: Andrea Schneider

Printed in the United States of America, North Mankato, MN.

TABLE OF
CONTENTS

A DANGEROUS JOURNEY!

THE NETHER

Two friends are going on a *Minecraft* adventure. First, they choose their **skins**. One plays as Steve, and the other plays as Alex. Next, the players check their supplies. They wear armor and weapons. They carry flint and steel to spark light. Now they are ready to visit the Nether.

The players build an entrance to this dark, rugged area. It is filled with lava and fire. Dangerous **mobs** could attack at any time. *Minecraft* is full of exciting places to explore!

ALEX

STEVE

BUILDING NEW WORLDS

CONSOLES

Minecraft is a video game developed by Mojang Studios. Mojang's **headquarters** is in Stockholm, Sweden. This popular **sandbox game** can be played on computers, **consoles**, and mobile devices. Players join **servers** to explore different worlds. They use blocks to build structures and craft items.

Outside of the game, people can attend events and collect *Minecraft* toys, clothing, and other items. With so much to offer, *Minecraft* continues to attract new fans. Millions of people play each month!

MOJANG HEADQUARTERS

STOCKHOLM, SWEDEN

EUROPE

Minecraft was created by Markus "Notch" Persson. Notch learned to program computers at a young age. He wrote his first computer game at age 8! As an adult, Notch enjoyed playing a block-building video game called *Infiniminer*. He decided to make a similar game.

INFINIMINER

In Notch's game, players mined materials and crafted things from them. This inspired the *Minecraft* name. Notch released the first version of *Minecraft* to the public in 2009. It was an instant hit! That year, Notch helped start a video game company called Mojang Studios. Its purpose was to further develop the *Minecraft* universe.

JUNGLE BIOME

SHELTER

The game begins in the Overworld. In early versions, players could explore several biomes, including a forest or desert. Today, there are more than 60 biomes. With every new update, more mobs, blocks, and crafting items are added!

Players can explore each biome. They gather materials such as wood, ore, or Nether wart. These are used to craft weapons, build shelters, and brew potions. Players may encounter friendly mobs such as farm animals or villagers. Hostile mobs, like creepers and ghasts, may attack. Players can fight them to collect special items!

HOW DO I LOOK?

Players can customize how Steve and Alex look. They can choose colors, outfits, hairstyles, and more!

EARLY MINECRAFT MOBS

MOB NAME	WHAT THEY DROP
▶ PIG ▶	PORK CHOPS
▶ SHEEP ▶	WOOL, MUTTON
▶ ZOMBIE ▶	ROTTEN MEAT
▶ SKELETON ▶	BONES, ARROWS, ARMOR, WEAPONS
▶ CREEPER ▶	GUNPOWDER, MUSIC DISKS

Mojang continued to add more dangers. Early on, players had to learn how to survive the night. They had to build shelters to protect themselves from monsters. By 2010, players could enter the Nether. There, they faced scary mobs, lava, and fire. The End was added in 2016. The fearsome Ender Dragon spawns on its central island!

SALES GROWTH

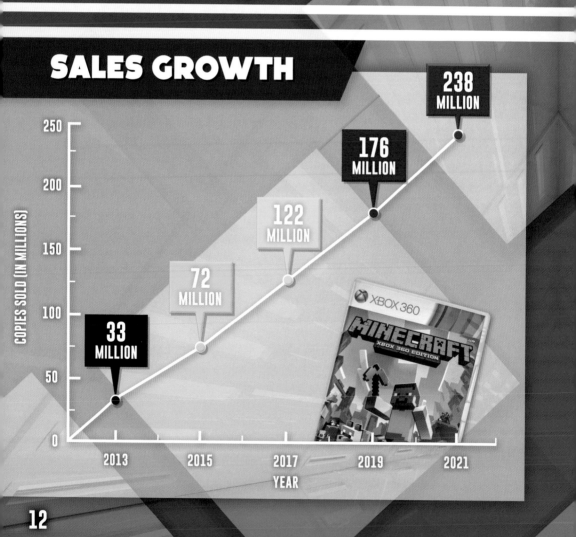

COPIES SOLD (IN MILLIONS)

33 MILLION

72 MILLION

122 MILLION

176 MILLION

238 MILLION

XBOX 360

MINECRAFT
XBOX 360 EDITION

2013   2015   2017   2019   2021

YEAR

ENDER DRAGON

Players loved the ever-changing *Minecraft* universe. The game sold millions of copies. Today, it is one of the most successful video games of all time!

MINECRAFT MODES

Players can choose how they want to play *Minecraft*. In Creative and Spectator modes, players explore different worlds free from danger. Those who want more challenge can play Survival, Adventure, or Hardcore mode.

MORE TO EXPLORE

MINECRAFT: POCKET EDITION

NINTENDO SWITCH

Minecraft faced changes in its early years. In 2011, Jens Bergensten became the game's lead designer. He and his team worked to expand the game to other **platforms**. *Minecraft: Pocket Edition* was soon launched for mobile devices. People could play *Minecraft* on the go! In the years that followed, the game also became available on consoles such as Xbox, PlayStation, and Nintendo Switch.

In 2014, a company called Microsoft bought Mojang for $2.5 billion. *Minecraft* continued to grow in popularity. In 2015, Mojang worked with Telltale Studios to release *Minecraft: Story Mode*, an adventure game based on *Minecraft*. In this game, players could solve puzzles to fight enemies!

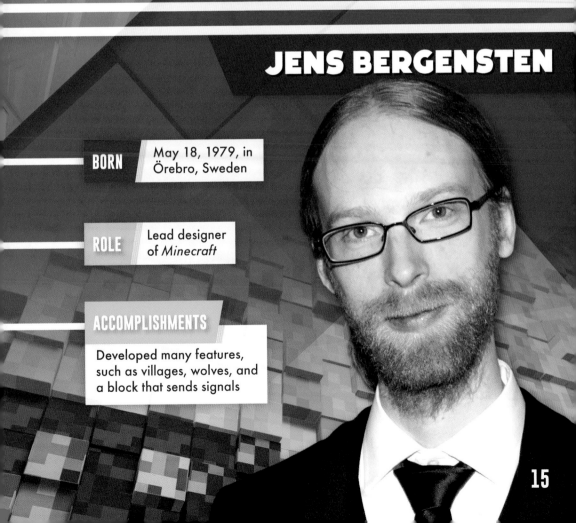

JENS BERGENSTEN

BORN May 18, 1979, in Örebro, Sweden

ROLE Lead designer of *Minecraft*

ACCOMPLISHMENTS

Developed many features, such as villages, wolves, and a block that sends signals

Over time, Mojang continued to add new features to *Minecraft*. Some additions, such as vegetables, were small. Others changed the game in big ways. Shipwrecks and dolphins were added in a 2018 update. In 2019, blast furnaces were added. These help players quickly melt ore to make tools and gear.

PET MOBS

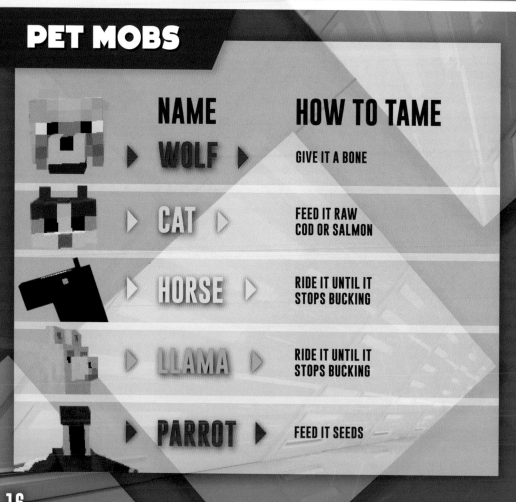

	NAME	HOW TO TAME
	▶ WOLF ▶	GIVE IT A BONE
	▶ CAT ▶	FEED IT RAW COD OR SALMON
	▶ HORSE ▶	RIDE IT UNTIL IT STOPS BUCKING
	▶ LLAMA ▶	RIDE IT UNTIL IT STOPS BUCKING
	▶ PARROT ▶	FEED IT SEEDS

AXOLOTL

GLOW SQUID

In 2021, the Caves & Cliffs update was released. It added snow-capped mountains, lush caves, and underground lakes. New mobs also joined the game. Now, players could catch axolotls swimming in lush caves. They could spot glow squids swimming through the ocean!

MANGROVE SWAMP

FROGS

Today, playing *Minecraft* is as exciting as ever. Each update brings new biomes, mobs, and surprises. There is always more to discover! Frogs hop onto lily pads in mangrove swamps. Wolf-like creatures called miststalkers hunt in misty forests. They even howl at sunset!

Players who dare can enter the creepy Deep Dark. It lies deep beneath the surface of the *Minecraft* world. Players explore the ancient cities that spawn there. But they must watch out for wardens. They use sound to hunt prey!

WARDEN

In addition to game updates, Mojang continues to give players other new ways to enjoy *Minecraft*. In 2020, the company launched *Minecraft Dungeons*. This **dungeon-crawler game** does not feature mining or building. Instead, players explore dungeons and solve puzzles. They must avoid traps and battle monsters to complete the game.

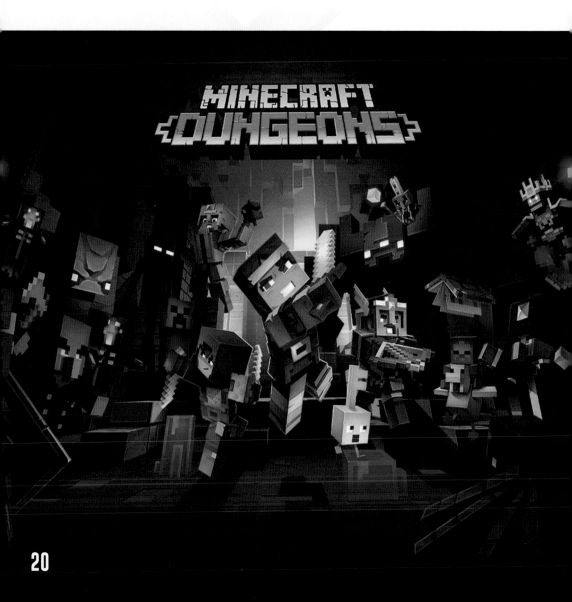

MINECRAFT TIMELINE

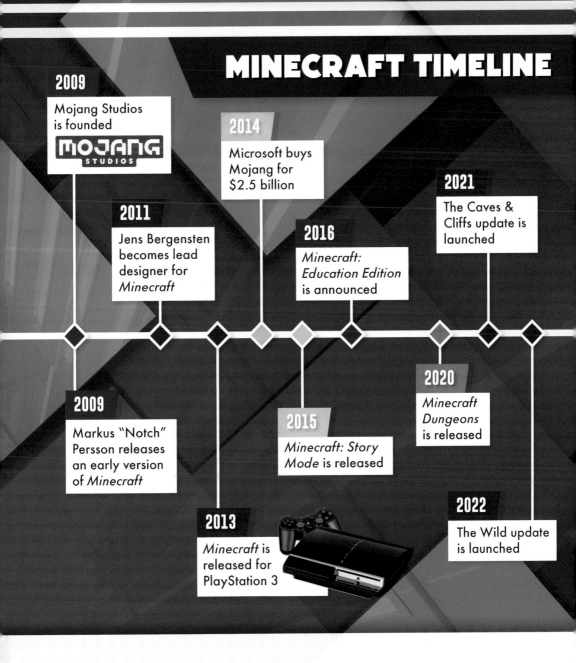

2009
Mojang Studios
is founded

MOJANG
STUDIOS

2014
Microsoft buys
Mojang for
$2.5 billion

2021
The Caves &
Cliffs update is
launched

2011
Jens Bergensten
becomes lead
designer for
Minecraft

2016
*Minecraft:
Education Edition*
is announced

2009
Markus "Notch"
Persson releases
an early version
of *Minecraft*

2015
*Minecraft: Story
Mode* is released

2020
*Minecraft
Dungeons*
is released

2013
Minecraft is
released for
PlayStation 3

2022
The Wild update
is launched

Minecraft Legends was released in 2023.
Players work in teams to defeat an invading
mob in this action-packed game. There is always
something new to discover in *Minecraft*!

BUILDING FOR CHANGE

CORAL REEF

MANGROVE SWAMP

Minecraft makes a difference outside of gaming. In 2018, Mojang gave $100,000 to protect coral reefs. That same year, they gave $200,000 to protect bees and pandas. In 2019, Mojang gave $100,000 to an organization called charity:water. This helped more than 3,000 people get clean drinking water.

In 2022, the Wild update added mangrove swamps to *Minecraft*. To go along with the update, Mojang promised to give $200,000 to help protect real mangrove forests.

GIVING BACK

$100,000
TO PROTECT CORAL REEFS IN 2018

$200,000
TO PROTECT BEES AND PANDAS IN 2018

$100,000
TO GIVE PEOPLE CLEAN WATER IN 2019

$200,000
TO PROTECT MANGROVE FORESTS IN 2022

Mojang has also teamed with the Block by Block Foundation to improve communities around the world. First, Block by Block recreates public spaces in *Minecraft*. Then, community members step in and add new features to it. Finally, builders use the completed model to build real-life improvements for the community.

RESTORED PLAY AREA
NAIROBI, KENYA

RESTORED WALKWAY
SÃO PAULO, BRAZIL

Mojang and Block by Block have helped dozens of communities complete exciting projects. They include a marketplace in Ghana, walkways in Brazil, and a play area in Kenya. *Minecraft* helps both people and the environment!

CRAFTING TOGETHER

MINECON
COSTUME

Fans enjoy *Minecraft* in many ways. In 2011, Mojang began hosting a **convention** called MineCon. Fans gathered to meet their online friends, learn about new *Minecraft* products, and play the game together.

In 2020, the event's name changed to *Minecraft* Live. This online convention lets fans across the globe enjoy *Minecraft* events from home. It includes game updates and news about developers. Fans can share ideas for how to enjoy the game. They can also vote for the next new mob!

MOB WINNER

Allay are one of *Minecraft*'s newest mobs. They were the winner of the *Minecraft* Live 2021 Mob Vote. Allay are small, blue, and can fly. They collect matching items and deliver them to players.

MINECRAFT LIVE

WHAT IT IS

An online *Minecraft* convention where fans get news and share ideas

FIRST HELD

2011 as MineCon

WHEN IT HAPPENS   Once every year

WHERE IT HAPPENS   Online

27

Some *Minecraft* fans enjoy creating **mods**. This lets them change the game in fun ways. They can change colors or add new items, mobs, or biomes. Vivecraft is a mod that changes *Minecraft* into a **virtual reality** experience. Players wear special headsets to enter the *Minecraft* world!

VIVECRAFT MOD

VIRTUAL REALITY HEADSET

MINECRAFT:
EDUCATION EDITION

PLAYING FOR PEACE

Minecraft Active Citizen is part of *Minecraft: Education Edition*. It introduces players to leaders who received Nobel Peace Prizes. Players work with the leaders to overcome challenges and build a more peaceful world!

Teachers around the world use *Minecraft: Education Edition* in their classrooms. Students can learn about science when they craft certain items. They can study geography by touring the Arctic on a dogsled or visiting ancient ruins. *Minecraft* allows people to build anything they can imagine!

GLOSSARY

biomes—large areas with certain plants, animals, and weather

consoles—electronic devices for playing video games

convention—an event where fans of a subject meet

dungeon-crawler game—an adventure game where players explore underground passages, solve puzzles, and face dangers

foundation—an organization that gives money to people or groups in need

headquarters—a company's main office

hostile—not friendly

mangrove—a tree or bush that grows in thick clusters along seashores and riverbanks

mobs—creatures that appear and move around in *Minecraft*

mods—short for modifications; mods are changes users make to the original game.

platforms—places to launch software, such as computers or video game consoles

sandbox game—a type of video game that is usually open-ended; sandbox video games often include tools that allow the player to change the game world.

servers—computer programs that allow people to play games together online

skins—images that determine what a character looks like in *Minecraft*

spawns—appears

virtual reality—computer technology that makes users feel like they are somewhere that does not really exist

TO LEARN MORE

AT THE LIBRARY

Keppeler, Jill. *The Inventors of Minecraft: Markus "Notch" Persson and His Coding Team*. New York, N.Y.: PowerKids Press, 2018.

Milton, Stephanie. *Minecraft For Beginners*. New York, N.Y.: Penguin Random House, 2019.

Schwartz, Heather E. *The World of Minecraft*. Minneapolis, Minn.: Lerner Publishing Group, 2018.

ON THE WEB

FACTSURFER

Factsurfer.com gives you a safe, fun way to find more information.

1. Go to www.factsurfer.com.

2. Enter "Minecraft" into the search box and click 🔍.

3. Select your book cover to see a list of related content.

INDEX

The images in this book are reproduced through the courtesy of: Pabkov, front cover, p. 5 (Steve); Zayacskz, front cover (Alex); Miguel Lagoa, front cover (smartphone); Jim McDowall/ Alamy, front cover (toy); Lego Photo mureut, front cover (LEGO); Cineberg Ug, front cover (toy shelves); Kseniya Golovina, p. 2; Roberto Bellomonte, pp. 3, 5 (Alex); Ben Molyneux/ Alamy, pp. 4-5; 8one6, p. 4 (Nether); Rokas Tenys, p. 6; Wachiwit, p. 6 (consoles); Nattee Chalermtiragool, p. 7 (Stockholm, Sweden); Zach Barth/ Zachtronics, p. 8 (*Infiniminer*); REUTERS/ Alamy, p. 9; Doc_js, p. 9 (jungle biome); Iurii Vlasenko/ Alamy, p. 10 (shelter); Kacher Hannes, p. 11 (Steve); Betsy Rathburn, pp. 11 (pig, sheep, zombie, skeleton, creeper), 16 (all), 17 (glow squid), 18 (mangrove swamp), 27 (allay); urbanbuzz, p. 12; Pe3k, p. 13; Thatirly79, p. 13 (Ender Dragon); Daniil Teslenko, p. 13 (mode); Pavel Kapysh, p. 14 (*Minecraft: Pocket Edition*); Info849943, p. 14 (Nintendo Switch); Lars Niki/ Getty Images, p. 15 (Jens Bergensten); mkfilm, p. 15 (blocks); SiPakne, p. 17 (axolotl); pngaaa, p. 19 (Warden); rafapress, p. 20; Wikipedia, p. 21 (2013); V_E, p. 22 (coral reef); balajisrinivasan, p. 22 (mangrove swamp); Block by Block team, pp. 24, 25; PA Images/ Alamy, p. 26; aslysun, p. 27 (*Minecraft* Live); Mike Prosser, p. 28 (Vivecraft mod); xiaorui, p. 28 (virtual reality headset); Bernhard Classen/ Alamy, p. 29 (*Minecraft: Education Edition*); lensfield, p. 29 (*Minecraft Active Citizen*); gersamina donnichi, p. 31 (pig, Steve).